Shadows in the Dawn

KATHRYN LASKY

Shadows in the Dawn
The Lemurs of Madagascar

PHOTOGRAPHS BY CHRISTOPHER G. KNIGHT

A GULLIVER GREEN BOOK

HARCOURT BRACE & COMPANY

San Diego   New York   London

Library of Congress Cataloging-in-Publication Data
Lasky, Kathryn.
Shadows in the dawn: the lemurs of Madagascar/written by Kathryn Lasky; photographs by Christopher G. Knight.
p. cm.
"Gulliver Green."
Includes bibliographical references.
Summary: Text and photographs follow primatologist Alison Jolly and a group of lemurs on the island of Madagascar, presenting the appearance, behavior, and social structure of these primates.
ISBN 0-15-200258-8   ISBN 0-15-200281-2 pb
1. Lemurs—Juvenile literature. [1. Lemurs. 2. Jolly, Alison.] I. Knight, Christopher G., ill.
II. Title.
QL737.P95L37   1998
599.8'3—dc21   97-6055

First edition
F E D C B A
F E D C B A (pb)

Printed in Hong Kong

We would like to thank Alison Jolly for including our family in the 1994 expedition to Berenty. We express our deep appreciation for her articulate and sensitive teaching style in the field. It was through her consummate skills as a teacher and scientist that the drama and fascination of the complex world of lemurs was revealed to us.

—K. L. and C. G. K.

Gulliver Green® books focus on various aspects of ecology and the environment, and a portion of the proceeds from the sale of these books is donated to protect, preserve, and restore native forests.

The display type was set in Esprit Book Italic.
The text type was set in Quadraat.
Color separations by Bright Arts, Ltd., Hong Kong
Printed and bound by South China Printing Company, Ltd., Hong Kong
This book was printed on totally chlorine-free Nymolla Matte Art paper.
Production supervision by Stanley Redfern and Pascha Gerlinger
Designed by Ivan Holmes and Lori McThomas Buley

To Linda Quan Knight and Jo Knight, companions
in adventure and superb primates in their own right

—K. L. and C. G. K.

Early Shadows

At the edge of a forest by a long winding river, in the first milky light of dawn, their silhouettes appear, moving slowly under the tamarind trees. They are thin and ragged, exhausted and wary.

Some have bald patches or torn ears, a slash wound on a hind leg or a missing tail tip. For lemurs the dry season is a terrible time. Food and water are scarce. Fights break out between troops. Weak members are often forced out of a troop and left to die alone.

This is also the season of birth. Between September, when a lemur is born, and January, the baby is too young for solid food and needs only its mother's milk. But if the mother is starving, the milk will not come and the baby will die. All of a mother's energy goes into eating so she can provide milk for the newborn that she carries on her back or that clings to her belly. A lemur mother has only one goal—to live so her baby may survive.

The seven members of this troop scatter into the thick underbrush to look for fallen tamarinds. Some settle for thick, prickly briers. Suddenly, however, they stop foraging and chewing and begin to mew. Their soft, low whines say, "I'm here . . . I'm here . . ." The lemurs mew because they sense an awful presence again; for days two females from outside the troop have been stalking them, harassing the mothers and chasing them away from the rest of the troop. The two females desperately want to belong to a troop—without one, they have no one to fight for them, to defend their territory, or to find and share food with.

The baby moves from the mother's back to her belly

and clings to her fur. Now the infant is hidden, except for its ring-patterned tail, which curls up like a little scroll. The troop keeps mewing and drawing closer together.

Suddenly two ragged females, one with a deep slit in her ear, the other with a partly bald tail, bound out of the brush. Their amber eyes blaze in the soft morning light. Loud yapping noises come from everywhere. The mother with the baby leaps in a lofty arc from the clump of cactus to a slender branch of a nearby tree; then an aerial loop brings her to a higher branch in another tree. She is near the forest canopy. Weighing just a few ounces, the baby clings while its mother flies from branch to branch. The other troop members cut off the two intruding females.

Within two minutes it is over. The mother and baby are safe. The strangers have been chased off—at least for now.

Only one of every two lemurs survives its first year of life in this tamarind forest on the island of Madagascar, formally known as the Malagasy Republic. Yet the forest, now a reserve, is the safest place in the world for infant lemurs. Within one square mile of this reserve live nearly five hundred ring-tailed lemurs. Madagascar, called the Red Island because of the color of its soil, is the only place on earth where lemurs can be found in the wild.

In this forest by the river there are numerous species of lemurs—the tiny mouse lemur that comes out only at night, the brown lemur, the sifaka that bounces on its hind legs, the night-wandering lepilemur that sleeps in tree hollows by day but can be spotted at night making spectacular leaps between vertical tree trunks like a small, moonlit acrobat.

Like humans, lemurs arc primates, mammals that share certain common traits, such as hands that are good at grasping, brains that are large in comparison to body size, and eyes that face forward to allow good depth perception. Millions and millions of years ago primates were very similar. But as with all living things, both plants and animals, life-forms change over time. This slow change is called evolution.

Within the primate family many smaller divisions evolved. Lemurs belong to a division known as prosimians, the most ancient primate group. They began to evolve more than fifty million years ago, at the dawn of the age of primates.

Prosimians' noses are moist, furless, and slightly longer than those of their fellow primates in the ape family. A prosimian's eyes are proportionately larger than

those of other primates, which gives it good night vision. They have large, flexible ears and special scent glands. Many of these features make prosimians fit for a nocturnal life, in which sound and smell count as much as sight.

Although prosimians share many features, they are different in small ways and are therefore separated into even more specific groups, or suborders. Tarsiers, lorises, pottos, bush babies, and lemurs are all suborders within the prosimian group.

The word *lemur* is derived from the Latin for ghost, perhaps so named because of the lemur's nocturnal habits. And whether the animal is the size of a mouse or a cat, whether it has brown fur or black fur, pointy ears or round ears, rings on its tail or a great ruff of golden fur around its neck, whether it bounces on its hind legs or runs on four—all are considered lemurs.

What makes a lemur a lemur rather than a loris or a tarsier? Some scientists believe the difference is based on certain details of the lemur's inner ear and characteristics

of the long twisted strands of DNA molecules that contain the instructions that make each living thing unique. Others think the matter is much more simple, believing that a lemur is a lemur because it lives on the Red Island, and of all the prosimians, only the lemurs dared to step onto the floating logs and branches and raft across the Mozambique Channel. Today there is an immense dent in the coastline of Kenya where Madagascar once was—for it was not always an island, but once was part of the continent of Africa. And then a very long time ago, 175 million years ago, the continent of Africa broke.

Accidental Pilgrims

One hundred thirty-five million years later, the lemurs floated across the water on logs, branches, perhaps even thick mats of seaweed, to reach the island. Earlier the journey might have been just a hop, for it takes a very long time for a piece of land to unhitch itself from another. Madagascar moved away from the east coast of Africa at the rate of about one inch a year. When the lemurs began their raft trips, Madagascar had drifted 231 miles from the African shore.

It was a big trip, and many other mammals did not go. Elephants would have been too heavy to raft across, but what about wild dogs or lions? Most mysterious of all, why, among all the primates, were the lemurs the only ones to dare the trip?

It was important for the lemurs to be the only ones. On the continent of Africa and elsewhere in the Northern Hemisphere where fossils of ancestral lemurs have been found, they were constantly outwitted by larger-brained primates such as monkeys and apes. All the prosimians—the lemurs, the tarsiers, the lorises, the pottos, the bush babies—were forced to stay in a nocturnal existence, giving the day to the brash upstart primates.

Without competition from their more quick-witted cousins, the lemurs had the run of the island. Only on Madagascar were they free to move out of the night and explore the day, to live in groups, to build nests, to find new habitats. They spread into places and ate and behaved in ways they had never before dared.

At that time, millions of years ago, there were almost fifty lemur species on Madagascar, some as small as mice and others as big as Saint Bernard dogs. Many of these have become extinct because humans, who arrived on

Madagascar fifteen hundred years ago, hunted them and changed their habitat. Now there are only about thirty known species.

Lemurs were not the only living things that made it to the new island. Before the lemurs left Africa, many reptiles had traveled to Madagascar when the trip was still short and they barely got their feet wet. Dinosaurs strolled to the island when the way was probably just a muddy path, and the boa constrictor slithered over at some point, leaving its niche in Africa open for the python.

But as the island moved farther away from the coast of Africa, fewer pilgrims attempted the crossing, especially the more newly evolved species. Staying behind with the monkeys and apes were salamanders, newts, toads, and poisonous snakes. They all missed their chance and never made the journey.

Yet many unusual plants and animals did evolve on the island and are found nowhere else on earth. The *Pachypodium*, chubby and lumpy and looking much like the elephant foot it's named for, bursts into bright yellow blossoms at the end of the dry season. The rosy periwinkle holds in its roots a treasure that is used to make medicine to treat childhood leukemia. A tree called the baobab can live more than a thousand years. There are weird insects, such as the walking flower, which in its youngest form looks like a snowy explosion of feathery threads and as an adult resembles the petals of a rose. There are cockroaches that hiss and more than fifty kinds of chameleons and lizards, one like a miniature dragon and another that can fit on the end of a person's thumb. All of these creatures, along with thirty different species of lemurs, live only on Madagascar and its smaller surrounding islands.

Yet this magical place is disappearing—minute by minute, hour by hour, the great Red Island, the fourth largest island in the world, the island on which these strange and wonderful creatures live, is dissolving into the sea. The erosion of the red soil makes Madagascar look as if it is bleeding into the Indian Ocean. In order for the humans to clear land for growing food, forests have been cut down and burned. Burned land without trees cannot hold the soil, so it washes away a bit more every day. One day there may not be enough topsoil to grow food for people or to anchor the trees that provide habitats for the lemurs. And someday the lemurs could truly become ghosts in their own land.

Searchers at the Dawn

There's Sally over in that clump of cactus. I bet Calm Mom and her infant are near," Hari says.

"There they are, Hari, other side!" calls Haja.

"Eating kily at standard ten to twenty meters apart."

"Oh, dear, Calm Mom is starting to mew. Slit Ear and Girt must be closing in . . ."

"How long have they been eating here?" Alison asks, just arriving.

One of the young researchers looks at her watch and makes a mark on a clipboard. "Four minutes here in this kily." *Kily* is another word for tamarind. "But Girt and Slit Ear are coming up."

"That hasn't been settled yet?" Alison sighs deeply.

"No." The Malagasy students laugh and shake their heads. Just then a burst of loud yapping erupts.

"Fight!" The researchers sprint through the spiny forest growth. Cactus needles tear at their clothes as they try to follow the lemurs, who have begun a wild aerial chase through the tops of the tallest tamarind trees. In seconds, it is all over.

"Here come John Wayne and Buddy!" calls Alison as the male lemurs break into fierce howls. She smiles. "So at last the guys show up!"

Alison leaves the students to their observations and walks up through the forest to the area called Piccadilly, where many paths cross and a water trough has been placed for the lemurs. She scratches her head, musing. "How long has this fracas with Slit Ear and Girt and the Leonardo troop been going on now—two weeks? You would have thought they'd have worked it out by now." Just what is going on in this troop? Why aren't Girt and Slit Ear definitely in or out? Why isn't Calm Mom or one of the other mothers taking a stand against the intruders, and why are John Wayne and Buddy so slow to help? Frightened

mothers, jealous outsiders, lazy males. This troop problem is turning into a big family crisis.

Family crises like these fascinate Alison Jolly, who has been studying lemur families for more than thirty years. She is a primatologist. Like paleontologists, primatologists are interested in the very distant past of millions of years ago. Paleontologists look for evidence of ancient life through fossils. Although primatologists do not look for actual fossils, in a sense they seek fossil behaviors by observing lemurs or chimpanzees or monkeys, whose histories spiral back to the dawn of the primate age.

Just as astronomers use telescopes to scan the sky for clues to the origins of our universe, Alison peers into the lives of lemurs for clues about the evolution of primate life on earth and the story of our own human family. She studies how mothers learn to mother and how fathers learn to father. How children learn to play. How the story of behavior unfolds. She is truly a searcher at the dawn. And she feels an enormous amount of pressure, because of the risk that her subjects might vanish into thin air.

The Dinosaur That Was Bigger Than the Living Room

When I was a little girl living in an apartment in New York City, my mother brought home a dinosaur book one day. We began reading it, and when we got to the bit about the diplodocus being the longest dinosaur in the world, with a length of seventy feet, I didn't know how long that was. So I asked and my mother said that was three and one-half times longer than our living room. I was absolutely pop-eyed. Why, the biggest dragon I had ever imagined was only two times bigger than our living room!"

Alison decided right then to become a scientist. She was in second grade. Her logic was simple: If she really wanted to be astonished, constantly, science was the only choice.

But she became a primatologist by accident. In college she studied zoology and later began a study of sponges. She liked marine biology, to snorkel and explore reefs, so studying sponges seemed like a good choice. Yet after a couple of years she became bored with her underwater subjects.

One day Alison saw a picture of a tarsier, with its enormous eyes and little hands with long fingers that grasped and clung. It was furry and dear and cute, a lot cuter than a sponge. She found out that in the anthropology department of Yale University, where she was studying, the first collection of live prosimians to come to America had just arrived, so she rushed over. And there she saw pottos and bush babies and lorises and tarsiers and lemurs!

"I looked at them. There were so many different kinds: little ones, big ones, little bigs and big littles, nocturnal and diurnal ones, fruit eaters, leaf eaters, insect eaters. Sponges are wonderful, but this . . . this was something else. Every way of life was possible for a prosimian. Just imagine, dial me up a nocturnal leaf eater who lives in tree hollows. It was as if you could begin to imagine alternate worlds. I rather enjoyed imagining a time when things might have gone a different way. Suppose, for example, monkeys had never evolved—well, would we all be lemurs? Possibly."

For Alison, who had been astonished by dinosaurs bigger than her living room in New York City and who grew up imagining other worlds, there was only one place to go—Madagascar.

A Last Refuge

There is a woodland in the oxbow of an old lake. Over the years it has grown into a rich forest that forms a corridor along the Mandrare River. Often called a gallery forest, it is set like a balcony high above the riverbank. When the de Heulme family arrived in Madagascar in 1936, they carved out from the wild desert land a plantation for raising sisal, a plant used to make rope. They treasured the rich tamarind forest that lined the river and delighted in the acrobatics of the ring-tailed lemurs and the sifakas. They saw what was happening to Madagascar and decided to protect this forest and its inhabitants by making it into a reserve, which they called Berenty.

The Antandroy tribal people share the tamarind forests and the spiny desert with the lemurs and other animals. For centuries these people have wound their way through the trees. To them the forest is everything—their medicine chest, their pantry, and their home. If they destroy the forest it is not because they do not value it, but because they value it too much and use all of its resources, for they are a desperately poor people. Since Berenty was made into a reserve many of the Antandroy people have been hired by the de Heulme family as guardians of the forest. Lemurs are no longer hunted.

The guardians glide silently through the forest, barefoot, often wrapped in colorful cloth *lambas*, or perhaps wearing just trousers or a loincloth and a dark blanket draped across one shoulder. They carry spears and will report anyone who harms the animals or the plants of the forest. Some work as guides, helping the researchers and the few tourists who come to view the lemur troops. One of the highest paid workers in the region, a guardian or guide can earn fifteen dollars a month.

It is to Berenty that Alison Jolly has come at least once a year since 1963 to study lemurs.

Until Alison began her studies, few people knew much about lemurs, and some of what they claimed to know was wrong. Many primatologists believed that female lemurs, like female chimpanzees and gorillas, were docile and dominated by the males. Alison believed that, too—until she met Aunt Agatha.

The Lesson of Aunt Agatha

It was 1963. Alison had been following a troop for several days and was used to the cantankerous ways of the old hag of a lemur she had named Aunt Agatha. Suddenly she saw Aunt Agatha bound toward the troop's dominant male, who was holding a lovely ripe tamarind. Silently she raised an arm and cuffed him hard on the nose, then grabbed the fruit. Alison was as stunned as the male and expected him to retaliate. Instead he meekly retreated and went in search of another fruit.

Alison was baffled. The male, called Vercingetorix, was strong, bold, and held high rank in the troop. He enjoyed lording over the others, so why would he tolerate such outrageous behavior from this female? All the primate studies at the time reported male lemurs as dominant over females. But had anyone really watched? Had they looked and followed, the way Alison had been doing for days now, through tamarind forests and into the spiny desert country inland from the river? Aunt Agatha's behavior opened Alison's eyes.

Alison observed the behavior again and again, not only in Aunt Agatha but in other females as well. The females were the bosses, dominating the troop. Nobody had looked carefully enough before. But Alison was looking all the time.

After Aunt Agatha cuffed him, Vercingetorix pulled the corners of his mouth back into a teeth-baring grimace and made strange squeaking sounds. The bared teeth might have looked warlike and combative, yet it was just the opposite. Alison realized that this expression was a signal of submission, apology, and even fright.

Alison calls the squeaking sound and its accompanying gesture a spat. The more she watched, the more she understood how the high-ranking females dominated the entire troop. On several occasions the males absolutely cowered before the females. In one gesture, which Alison calls a deep spat, a totally frightened and humiliated male lemur presses his nose right into the scolding female's face.

Alison observed another behavior that fascinated her—stink fights. Despite their funny name, they are not a game. Male lemurs have scent glands: one in each armpit and one on a large furry tuft, called a spur, on the inner surface of each forearm. When a lemur prepares for a stink fight he rubs his long tail along these scent-producing glands until the tail becomes good and smelly. Then he is ready to fight.

First the lemur faces off and gives his opponent a long hard stare. His amber eyes narrow to golden slits. His muzzle flares and his ears flatten. Then he begins to wave his long fluffy tail over his head, wafting the scent in the direction of the opponent.

That is all there is to a stink fight. It is a safe strategy, for no one can get hurt. When lemurs really fight, it is fast and bloody—they jump high into the air to deliver a devastating slash with their sharp canine teeth, which tear through flesh like nails. The old saying "Sticks and stones may break my bones, but words will never hurt me" can be paraphrased for lemurs: "Slashing teeth can cause me grief, but stinky smells won't hurt me."

From dawn to dusk, year in and year out, Alison followed the lemurs through the great tamarind forests and out onto the spiny desert. She wrote down and counted who cuffed whom, who occupied the best feeding positions, who got spatted or deep spatted and for what reasons. She recorded endless stink fights. Eventually a pattern of behavior began to emerge. Male lemurs were great at swaggering about, striking poses, flaring their muzzles, and making threats, but the real power rested with the females. They made fewer threats, but they delivered on them more often with a cuff. It was the high-ranking females who directed the troop.

Leonardo's Troop

*T*he researchers begin the day at dawn by scanning the treetops for the tails that hang down like fat, fuzzy caterpillars. Hari and Haja are Malagasy college students from Antananarivo, the capital of Madagascar; Carrie is a student from an American university. They have come to assist Alison in the field for a season.

To do their jobs the young women carry compasses, watches, and check sheets on clipboards. They mark their check sheets with the position of the troop and note which animal is doing what to whom.

"*Voilà! Voilà les queues en haut,*" Hari calls out and points directly overhead; she spots several ring-tailed lemurs forty feet up a kily tree.

The two other women join her and wait patiently. The animals are too high and the light too dim for them to observe any specific behavior, but they know that soon the lemurs will descend.

"Here they come."

"Oh, look. *Ça c'est Calm Mom, n'est-ce pas?* Here's Calm Mom." Alison has arrived. With the young women she speaks a mixture of French and English. Alison is fluent in French, but the Malagasy students are anxious to practice English. "Any sign of Slit Ear or Girt?" she asks.

"Not yet."

Although the students have been at Berenty for less than two weeks, they have quickly learned to distinguish between the animals. At first glance lemurs might seem identical, but as one becomes familiar with them, individual markings can be spotted. One animal might have a notch in his ear, another a slit in hers. They become Notch and Slit Ear. The star on a lemur's forehead might have a distinctive size and shape. The male for whom this troop is named has been called Leonardo after the great Italian

artist Leonardo da Vinci; the large star on his forehead is formed like a figure from a famous Leonardo work of art. Another male in this troop is called John Wayne because his unusually big wrist spurs make him appear to swagger like the famous cowboy actor. Researchers look for unique features and use nicknames so they can instantly identify a particular animal.

"*Regardez! Elles sont séparées*—they have separated!" Alison points to a leafy branch where Calm Mom is foraging with her baby. The baby has just popped off the mother's back to explore the limb on its own.

For the first month of its life, the baby never leaves its mother and is carried everywhere, plastered to either her back or her belly. Like a human infant, a newborn lemur can clutch with its hands, push with its arms, and cuddle up to its mother. The tummy-to-chest contact is very familiar to all primates, whether human, chimp, or lemur.

Just as human babies grow stronger and more curious by the day, so do lemurs. When it is about six weeks old, a lemur will get up the nerve to spring off its mother's body, if only for a few seconds. As the lemurs jump off and back on, they remind Alison of popcorn. With round heads like Ping-Pong balls, arms and legs like pipe cleaners, and tails like corkscrews, they go about their explorations. Each time, they grow a little bolder and venture a little farther from the mother, though they will not be fully independent for two years.

"Look," says Alison, "that baby is playing. It's pretending to eat a leaf." Infant lemurs only nurse at this age, so this baby is imitating its mother's eating. At six weeks old, lemurs already know how to pretend!

Play is the most important thing a lemur infant can do, Alison tells the students. Play is practice for life—for eating leaves, for fighting, for traveling through the treetops, for all the things a lemur must learn in order to survive.

Calm Mom's baby separates from her four times within fifteen minutes. The baby is daring and strong because, like a good human mother, Calm Mom knows how to care for, teach, cuddle, and protect her infant.

"But what really makes a good lemur mother," says Alison, "is for the mother to be healthy herself so she will have lots of milk, to help her baby grow strong and begin to pop off her body like popcorn, to play and then begin to fly through the trees, just like her mother."

The lemur daughters remain within the troop to help their mothers with the newborns until they have children of their own to care for. Sometimes they stay in the same troop and sometimes they join another, depending on the size of the troop.

The Leonardo troop begins to descend from the trees. With their tails held high over their heads like S's, they begin a slow parade up a forest path toward a water trough at a spot called Kily Junction.

"John Wayne and Buddy are together," Hari notes.

"Calm Mom and Other Mother seem to be at the center here with their babies—Calm Mom's infant has popped again!" Haja reports.

By the time the lemurs reach the water trough, the configuration has changed. The researchers note who feeds near whom and for how long, who moves off as another comes near, who gets to drink first.

"Uh-oh . . . here comes Van Gogh," Carrie says. A large lemur with a torn ear, a member of another troop, makes his way toward the water trough. He boldly displaces Buddy and Other Mother, who quickly move off.

"Genital marking!" Hari calls, and writes on her check sheet. "Calm Mom did it. Ah, now Buddy genital marks!"

Both animals have backed up against bushes near the trough and rubbed their rear ends against the branches to leave their scent. The scent marks are like territorial signposts, warning invading lemurs like Van Gogh that this is not their place; the Leonardo troop was here first.

Calm Mom quickly moves in on Van Gogh, who is still at the trough.

"Would you look at her!" Alison marvels. A loud howl comes from down the path, a sound only male lemurs make. It means, "I am here, I am male, and I am tough." But the howl comes too late. Calm Mom has already threatened Van Gogh. Alison laughs as the howler approaches. "Oh, here, finally Leonardo shows up. The wimp!"

After a quick drink, however, Leonardo begins to swagger and rub his tail through his wrist spurs. He moves toward a glaring Van Gogh, then Buddy steps into the path and interferes. The stink fight is over before it begins. Van Gogh moves off. He will return when this troop is finished at the water trough. A conflict has been avoided. Lemurs are better than many primates at making peace. They know how costly a violent fight can be.

The lemur's mating season lasts for just two weeks in April. Early in her research, Alison began to form a hunch that the shortness of the mating season might be why male

lemurs rarely fight intensely. Only during the mating time do male lemurs give up on harmless stink fights and have serious fights in which they slash with their teeth. A female is only fertile for a few hours, and there is fierce competition by the males to determine who will be her mate. Even in groups of animals in which males do very little parenting, the males have an urge to reproduce; it is the only way their bloodlines may be carried into future generations. So during these two weeks in April the males become extremely ferocious and will seriously fight other males. After April, the worst of the competition is over. The male lemurs have the rest of the year to settle their differences peaceably.

For female lemurs, however, it is different. Being a good mother means protecting a newborn through the harsh dry season and then watching over it for the next two years. A female lemur most often fights for her children. She fights for the best food for herself as a nursing mother, then for her offspring when they are weaned and have outgrown nursing. Sometimes this means staking out the best place at the water hole or the best tree in the forest. The females must be strong and dominant for more than just two weeks a year. Alison believes this is why the females are the power center of a troop. For a female, it pays to be a fighter almost all year long. For a male, fighting can be a waste of time and energy.

Just before Van Gogh moved away from the water trough, Alison and the students saw him grimace at Leonardo and Calm Mom. It was not quite a spat nor a true grin. For many years Alison has been fascinated with the relationship between smiling and fear in primates. Chimpanzees have many different grins, some for fear, some for begging, others for greeting.

For lemurs, too, the pulled-back mouth that may look like a grin rarely represents joy. It often indicates submission and sometimes fear; expressing such emotions can be an important negotiating tool in threatening social situations. A truly frightened lemur uses other signals and alarms. A high-intensity scream is an air-raid alarm against hawks or eagles, which are among the few predators of lemurs. For danger on the ground, lemurs make a yapping sound.

The different shades of a grimace, the wave of a tail, the cries that range from howls to screams to mews are all gestures and sounds that are part of the intricate web of communication that draws lemurs into social groups.

Together they must share a forest, forage for food, defend territory, breed, and raise their young. It seems impossible to imagine that before the African continent divided, before lemurs made their raft trips to the new island, lemurs were solitary nocturnal creatures—animals who lived independently and never ventured into the day. Over the last forty million years they have evolved, becoming highly social, with systems for communicating and keeping order within their troops.

In the heat of the day, when the lemurs rest like balls of fur high in the shadowy foliage of the tamarind trees, Alison returns to her cabin to map the troops' movements. She has a computer-generated graph of the entire Berenty Reserve that marks every tree, identifying what kind it is and whether it is dead or alive. With colored pencils she has outlined the day ranges of the various troops, using a different color to represent each one. She can see a troop's boundaries and where it overlaps with other troops. Alison needs to know this so people might better understand how the reserve can be managed, how it can support both the lemurs and the people who live there. The reserve is like a laboratory for the rest of the country.

The threat to Madagascar is that its topsoil will some-

day bleed into the Indian Ocean and the island will become a treeless rock that can give life to nothing. But Alison dreams of a future in which lemurs and people will be able to live together. For her dream to come true, Alison must continue to study the lemurs and how they live within their troops and how their troops move through the land.

The Spiny Desert

The lemurs do not always live within the shade of the tamarind forest. Sometimes troops venture out into the spiny desert. It is not unusual to see a ring-tailed lemur or a sifaka nestling among the sharp spikes and needles of the thorny plants that bristle out of the sandy earth.

The desert is a prickly maze and each variety of plant is unique. The *Alluaudia procera* strikes high into the sky, its long fingers covered with spirals of spines. Its relative *Alluaudia ascendens* is covered with small spiked knobs. *Didierea trolli*, with its twisted tentacles, is also called the octopus tree. Each of these plants or trees has its own odd geometry of thorns that is organized in patterns so the leaves will not be easily eaten by hungry animals.

It is amazing that any animal can find refuge in such a hostile place. But for some reason either the thorns do not cut the lemurs or the lemurs know how to jump among them without getting hurt. To human observers, watching the sifakas and ring-tailed lemurs leap and prance through this vicious maze seems as neat a trick as dancing between raindrops without getting wet.

At night the spiny forest becomes an even stranger place. The skeletal fingers of the *Alluaudia procera* sway in the evening breeze and seem to scrape the cobweb clouds that hang across the moon. The baobabs swell like immense gray balloons inflated against the night. An armored chameleon freezes in a flashlight's beam, a dusty knight back from battle. And deep within a bristling web of branches nestles the mouse lemur, the tiniest primate of all.

Spite and Death

There is trouble in troop A1. The problem is Jessica. For some reason she has been targeted by Fan and Fish, a mother and daughter, perhaps because a shake-up in troop ranks has created a power vacuum at the top.

Alison's students have followed this troop for many years. They know all the adult lemurs well—Fish, Fan, Finch, Bush, Kid, Scout, Jessica, and Locket. They know the family trees. Jessica and Locket are sisters, and daughters of a high-ranking female, Diva, who died last year. Locket now has two daughters of her own: a juvenile, Pele, named after the Hawaiian goddess of the volcano because her eyes are as red as fire, and an infant. Pele often helps her mother care for the new baby. Kid also has a baby. Kid and Scout are sisters, and the daughters of Bush, a high-ranking female. Then there are the adult males—Fang, Milton, Geek, and Buck—and three juveniles, Kai, Kele, and Prince. There is one subadult, or near adult, a male called Bart.

Bush and Kid, mother and daughter, are now the dominants. But Fish and her family are turning into terrorists. The males are on the edge of this drama; the females have been trying to work out the conflict over the past five weeks. And the researchers are observing, trying to answer a very important question: Is high rank and dominance passed from one generation to the next? If so, Jessica, Locket, Scout, and Kid, as the daughters of high-ranking females, should become the troop leaders. But things are shaky. Old ways seem ready to topple.

"Fish and Fan," says Alison, "are acting like typical midrank aggressors on the rise. There's been a shake-up with the death of Diva. They want to get to the top."

When the researchers arrive, Fish and Fan are literally starving Jessica out of the troop. Every time Jessica comes near they make it impossible for her to get food, going out of their way to push her aside. This behavior is called spite or targeted aggression, because there is no immediate

profit for the aggressor. The animal must give up something to cause a problem for the victim. Spite usually has one goal: to drive a member from the troop so there will be a larger food supply for those who remain. Spite takes time and energy, and the rewards are not instant.

For a brief time Fish and Fan ease up on Jessica, then start in on Scout and Kid. The troop is jittery, and perhaps it is the nervousness and the pressures of spite that cause Kid's baby to fall. It happens as troop G2 approaches. Annie Oakley, a high-ranking G2 female, and another female charge Kid. As Kid retreats through the branches, the baby tumbles to the ground. Kid runs to rescue her infant, but Annie Oakley and her sidekick will not let her near. The baby becomes a hostage.

Kid and her mother, Bush, charge Annie Oakley and get the baby back. The baby, however, has been injured in the fall and is too weak to cling to his mother. Then the researchers see something no one has ever seen a lemur do. Kid picks up the baby with one foreleg and runs away on three legs. Three hours later they see something even more amazing: Kid walks across a forty-foot-high branch on two legs while she holds the baby.

A few hours later the baby falls a last time. He dies instantly.

Kid grieves for hours. She makes a strange crying sound; she holds and noses her baby's body. The others come. Fish and Fan actually try to run Kid off and hold the baby hostage in death as Annie Oakley had done in life. They would only dare do this to a low-status mother.

Is Kid's status falling by the minute? Fish and Fan leave after five minutes. Kid can hear the members of her troop retreating deeper into the forest. She mews. "I am here . . . I am here . . ." Her troop returns her calls to let her know where they are. Yet Kid cannot tear herself from the dead infant. Four hours pass. Fish suddenly reappears and displaces Kid from her baby. Is this pure spite, to come all the way from the deeper forest to push a mother away from her dead infant? Fish stays for a few moments and then retreats. The mother returns and sniffs the little limp body. She will stay with the infant into the night.

But finally the pull of the troop wins out. Kid must rejoin them. The night is too long to be alone.

On the Edge

*I*t is sunset. Across from the forest, Antandroy women stand knee-deep in the river as they wash their clothes. Their *lambas* blow in the breeze like bright pennants. A raft of snowy white egrets takes flight from the cocoa-colored water. And then on the near shore, a troop of lemurs descends from the forest to the water's edge to drink. Scout is in the lead, next is Locket with her baby, and close behind, Kid. Pele comes over to groom Locket's daughter. Kele and Prince give way to Scout. Fan and Fish arrive. Kid moves closer to Pele as if for protection.

Annie Oakley suddenly appears a few yards away. Fan takes note and immediately backs her rump against a rock and leaves a scent to say, "This is my drinking place." Annie Oakley runs off; Locket and her infant move away from Fan as well. Pele, however, the daughter of Locket, does not move. She raises her muzzle, her red eyes glaring directly at Fish and Fan.

The sun sinks beneath the horizon. Low thin purple clouds swim like eels across the sky. As the shadowy lemurs slide through the twilight, the troop's black-and-white markings fade into the dusky light, the white stars on their faces blurring into their bandit masks.

And the eyes of Pele glow like two live coals in the Madagascar night.

Afterword

Alison Jolly earned her doctorate at Yale University and currently teaches at Princeton University. She has written numerous books and magazine articles about primate behavior and the evolution of human behavior, and has been featured on several television programs. She is the former president of the International Primatological Society.

When Alison first went to Madagascar there were fewer than thirty known species of lemurs. Since then several new species have been found, including the golden crowned sifaka, the golden bamboo lemur, the hairy-eared dwarf lemur, and the pygmy mouse lemur.

Madagascar is a country in crisis. As the population of Madagascar increases and as more forests are slashed and burned to create cropland, the lemur habitat is vanishing. This is not just bad for lemurs; it is bad for every living thing. If the forests are not properly managed, firewood will run out, the watershed will evaporate, and no life will be supported.

The more Alison learns about lemur behavior, about how much social and physical space a troop of lemurs requires, the more she can help the Malagasy government plan for the future of its own people and understand how people and animals can live together in a supportable environment. The Wildlife Preservation Trust International is dedicated to helping with this task and many other preservation efforts.

For further information about the organization,
write to:
Wildlife Preservation Trust International
1520 Locust Street, Suite 704
Philadelphia, PA 19102
www.columbia.edu/cu/cerc/wpti.html

Further Reading

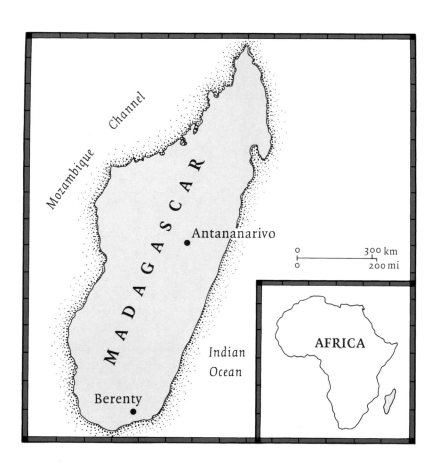

Durrell, Gerald. *The Aye-Aye and I: A Rescue Mission in Madagascar*. New York: Arcade Pub., 1993.

Jolly, Alison. "Madagascar Lemurs." *National Geographic*, August 1988.

Lanting, Frans. *Madagascar: A World Out of Time*. New York: Aperture Foundation, Inc., 1990.

Mittermeier, Russell A., Ian Tattersall, William R. Konstant, David M. Meyers, Roderic B. Mast, and Stephen D. Nash, illus. *Lemur Guide*. Washington, DC: Conservation International, 1994.